POETRY...
from the Colors of My Mind

SELENA HASKINS

PUBLISHING

DREAM WRITE PUBLISH

ISBN: 978-0-9859096-8-0
Library of Congress Control Number: 2018906949

Printed in the United States of America

Published by Calidream Publishing
Email: **selena@calidreampub.com**

For bookings visit: **www.booksbyselena.com**
Or email: **selena@calidreampub.com**

Cover Image by Artist Agsandrew @Shutterstock

Thanks to my loves: ♥ My husband and son. Love you guys to Life!

To Mom, thanks for reading my work and giving me the best review that an author/poet could ask for- honesty! ☐I love you to the moon and back.

To my family and friends who came out during those poetry nights in the 90s to hear me read, and who listened to my poems in the middle of the night when I was feeling some kind of way.

A big THANK YOU to all of my readers and everyone who continues to support me! Hug yourselves for me. *Squeeze*

I thank my team at Calidream Publishing. We're a very small group with giant hearts. ♥

Many thanks to my editor, Barbara Joe Williams. Book formatter- Karen Perkins at LionheART Publishing, and my beta readers, who gave me the green light to GO!

Dear Reader:

This is a collection of poems that I've written during my college years along with a few newer poems that I wrote in the middle of the night when the rest of the world was asleep... and I couldn't sleep. I've always used poetry to express my deepest thoughts, but I kept them to myself like a private journal. I was that girl on campus that you would see walking around with a composition book in her hand, ready to pen any experience that life allowed me to see, feel, taste, hear, smell or touch. These poems are pieces of me. Pieces of me when I was searching for love. Pieces of me when I found love. Pieces of me when I was hurt and broken. Pieces of me when I was lost and confused. Pieces of me that would eventually make me whole and turn me into the woman who God meant for me to be. I hope you enjoy this first volume. There's more to come.

Please check out my other published works:

· *Yesterday Was a Long Time Ago* (novel, 2017)

· *A River Moves Forward* (Part 1 -novel, 2013)

· *Riding the Waves* (Part 2- novel, 2014)

· *Just Between Us-Inspiring Stories by Women*
(collection of non-fiction short stories, 2013)

Contents

POETRY...
from the Colors of
My Mind

Forbidden Fruit

In the darkness, pleasures lie and spill forth fantasies of unwinding limbs, bending joints, flexed knees, and the sweet taste of nectar.

Strange fruit of a soft middle, signed in a promised vow, now broken by a Hung tree that grew wildly from a forest that explored every growing green, and deflowered each beautiful thing.

The heat of two souls steaming like a warm mist in a distinctive natural funk with feelings of bliss.

Their silhouettes are moving like earthworms, turning, spinning, crawling, begging, scratching until energy exhausts into thin air, and faints onto the bed.

But in the morning, the sun warms and awakens their souls.

Eyes wide open, seeing the truth for what it is; it stands erect, and what they see now is a hot mess!

No turning back the hands of time, where too much wine evoked deep feelings from within.

Lost, confused, perplexed, wondering what to do next. Last night was no dream, but they thought it was fun; now they wish it could be undone.

It's too late, the Light saw them in the darkness of their forbidden lust. They are fully awakened to their sins.

Good morning.

Grief

There is no defined emotion
that can describe a loss
but there is a unique understanding
of its common cause.

There is nothing anyone can say
that can ease the pain
time can be the only healer
while memories remain.

When everyone leaves today
tomorrow, I will question if this was real
it will hurt much more in the morning
when your absence sends me chills.

I will be left with nothing and no one
just a blanket of quiet sound
filled with wondering thoughts between sobbing
and wondering what to do now.

I will look out the window and see the mailman
delivering the mail
life will move on even in my sorrow
but my faith will make me well.

Forever Love

How deep is your love for me?
Right now, I am young, gentle, and green
but would you still love me if I lost my memory?

How deep is your love for me?
I'm smart, beautiful, and fit
but would you still love me if I needed prosthetics?

How deep is your love for me?
Right now, I still have all my hair and teeth
but would you still love me if I were bald and frail
with dentures and no real teeth?

How deep is your love for me?
Please don't just think about today
think about the future when my beauty and youth will
all fade away.

I Believe

I believe what you put out is what you get back
if you put out anger, you get a heart attack
if you put out negative vibes
you get back negative energy
and I've never been a person who created frenemies.

I believe that love is a healer for the world
I believe that hate is a stealer of peace
and if I don't forgive someone
I'm only hurting ME.

I believe that kindness should have its limits
otherwise, I'm just a giver; ain't no friendship in it.

I believe you should take care of yourself
you can't keep giving up YOU
or there won't be anything left.

I believe every mother should be given a good life
especially the single moms, who make the extra
sacrifice.

I believe every father should be given the fist pound
if he's a real man to his children
he should be given a crown.

I believe every elder deserves respect
they carry knowledge and wisdom
that keep us in check.

I believe Jehovah God created the universe
and how He meant for us to live forever and not die
from the curse.

I believe if we all believe, or at least try,
we can get through the storms and not have to die.

I believe, because the one thing I have is hope,
and as long as I keep living, my faith will help me to
cope.

I believe!

The Concrete Jungle

Welcome to the concrete jungle,
where a win or a loss happens on the asphalt
grinding in the rain
in the snow
under the hot sun
and on into the night
the hoopers can assault without a gun or a knife.

An elbow to the chin
the real hard defense
the kind you can't cry about
when you fall down, you get back up
ain't no calling timeout.

Welcome to the concrete jungle,
where even if there are no nets
you can hear the *Swish* of the three
and that's winning all bets!

Got no money? Your shirt is coming with me.
or your brand new sneakers will be mine
take them off your feet.

Welcome to the concrete jungle,
this is Watkins Playground
I own this court
playing with a bald Spalding with no lines on it
still beat anyone on the court.

This is the jungle, and my uncles taught me
how to play against the best of them
I sent them all crying to their Mamas and
walking with a limp.

The next day I go out to hoop it up again
preparing to take out all challengers
for that next win.

The jungle has always been my friend.

Coonin'

Sagging pants
Tight pants
Holey pants
Doing the dance
Coonin'

I won't tell
She won't tell
He won't tell
'cept for a price
to save ourselves
Coonin'

Yes'sir, Boss
Yes'sum, Mam'
He did that
She did that
We's sick boss
It's their loss
Not ours
But you're Coonin'

Fighting on TV for a buck
thinking you are winning
You're out of luck
Coonin'

Dancing and bragging
like the wealth is yours
but you are buying their brand names
what are you bragging for?
Coonin'
"I am black, and I am proud," you say
Oh, yeah?
Who are you fooling?
As far as I'm concerned, you're just Coonin'

As a Kid

I thought God was in my stomach
making me a tuna fish sandwich
Turned out, Mama was pregnant with my baby brother.
As a kid, I used to think that carnivals were strobe
lights, good music, card games, lots of people, and good
food ...
Turned out, it was my house.
As a kid, I thought every white man with a round belly
was Santa Claus or the police
Turned out, he was the landlord collecting rent money.
As a kid, I thought my cousin just liked playing dress
up in high-heels, and in skirts of his girl friends ...
Turned out, he would be the Queen of the night
and Spring Water was his lover and friend.
As a kid, I thought the nice painter, Mr. Billy, was just
tired and sleepy from work; he'd lean to the side and
almost fall down ...
Turned out, he was hooked on street pharmaceuticals
and died with little or no fanfare. They left him there.
As a kid, I thought Brock was a jerk!
He'd beat this woman black and blue
I grabbed my grandfather's gun and aimed it at him
She stopped me before I could shoot
And I realized at the age of ten that I wasn't a kid
anymore.

Conveniently Black

Everybody is black during the come up.
"Say, my brother, let's chop it up."

We cool. We real black. We laid back. We like that.

Everybody is black when we're in the same boat.
"Say, brother, what you need? Let's strike a barter for
them beans."

We cool. We real black. We laid back. We like that.

Everybody is black when we're in the hood.
"What's up, brother?"
"Ain't nothing; just chillin' and up to no good."

We cool. We real black. We laid back. We like that.

When we get rich, we jump ship.
"Say, brother, can I get a lift?"

Brother, we ain't cool. We ain't black. We mixed. We
ain't laid back on nothing; *I'm* the one who's rich.
Then we turn black again when Becky gets us in
trouble.
"Say, brother, protest my case cuz I ain't guilty."

"Nah, brother, we were real cool. We were laid back.
We were like that, but when I reached out my hand,
you didn't give back. You should never be conveniently
black."

Winter in America

Welcome! Welcome! Step right up
Are you a man or woman down on your luck?
Circling like a pigeon looking for crumbs
rubbing two pennies together with your sore thumbs
I am your Uncle Sam
your green eggs and ham
sign right here on the dotted line
you can have all the swine.

Winter has come in America
Watch her scold
Winter has come in America
to chastise the po'.
Now wait a minute, Mister, that ain't what I signed. I
can't read the fine print before that dotted line.
Ain't my problem, is it? this crap is yours to keep. You
take what I done gave you 'fore winter freezes your
baby's feet.
Save me, Uncle Sam, with more green eggs and ham.
My stomach is starving, and my baby is sick. Ole'
Mister gonna want his rent.
I'll sign again just to live. Save me, Uncle Sam
Save my kids.
I'm an educated man
fought for Miss America
with blood, sweat, and tears on her wings
Fifty stars and three stripes
It's winter in America, give me a life.

It's winter in America
I was hoping to be free.
It's winter in America
ain't no different in spring
It's winter in America
She ain't giving you a darn thing!

Window of My Eye

I don't know what I was thinking
I was just five years old
when the blood streamed down my cheeks.
Maybe I thought I was tough
I was definitely bossy enough
'til the boy in Congress Heights hit me with a bottle of
7-UP.

I could've gone blind, you know
I know that scar like it was yesterday
five stitches through my window
That's when the mole came
it was after he split my skull
"It's a beauty mark, child," Mom claimed.
So I never got rid of it. It's still the same.
I survived it though … that scar above my window.

I survived Congress Heights. Now you know.

Time Trapped in a Bottle

I wish I could trap time inside of a bottle
so I could keep you near
You would be my present,
my past, and a future I wouldn't fear.

If I could trap time in a bottle,
it would be filled with every yesterday
and the sun would shine upon your smile,
taking all your pain away.

But as time keeps on moving,
I can't trap it in
nor ink my feelings with a pen

All I have is the NOW
and that's good enough for me
because I will keep on loving you
as time just lets us be.

Orange Moon

I am an orange moon
Crowds cheer when I fly through mid-air
Sometimes I'm seen at night
Sometimes I'm seen during the day
I am the moving eyeball in the sky.
watch me sway.

I am an orange moon
Bats can't see me, but I can see them
I watch the bear sleep until spring
wake her up during March Madness
with sweet honey.

I am an orange moon
Full like a pumpkin with pimples
I captivate everyone's attention
for four quarters.

I am an orange moon
bouncing off cement
dribbling between long legs
flying through hands
and swishing through the nets.

I am an orange moon with eyes to the sky
lines around my body
scoring the last winning shot.
I am basketball.
SWISH!

Johari's Window

I sit and smile, not shedding a tear
but who is the one who knows my fear?
So deep is this silence, and they do not know
that everyone has a Johari's window
Though we may smile when we want to cry
or do something wild when emotions run high
Yet, we are careful that others don't see
for fear of being judged imperfectly
Sure, we have hearts and feelings we ride
but that part of self we choose to hide
The mirrors reflect the identities we know
but the fear of a man is the side he doesn't know
with no expressions to be expressed
He knows this is beyond his own intellect
So where he knows is where he returns
and settles in the place he discerned
As he walks, he examines his flow,
and it helps to remember his Johari's window.

If You Start to Wonder

If you start to wonder about the love I have for you
Think about the many ways of love I've shown to you
Think about the times I listened even when I was tired
Think about when I was there for you when your family
member died
Think about the support I gave you
When you tried to reach your goal
Think about my love for you
through the years, it has never eroded.
If you start to wonder about my love for you
Think about the dreams I sacrificed to be with you
Think about my loyalty and commitment I kept with
you
When other men asked me out
I never cheated on you
Think about the consideration and the care that I've
shown
when you were sick or feeling down
I stayed with you at home.
If you start to wonder about my love for you
I never put you down in public that was
between you and me.
If you start to wonder about my sincerity
Think about the times that I have shown true
humility
I have always been submissive
though I speak when I feel it's right
but I never yell at you or treat you impolite.

If you start to wonder about my love for you
I always treated you like a man and rendered you your
due.
If you keep on wondering whether my love for you is
true
it's time to look at yourself
I've played my part with you.

Winds That Pass Us By

I am standing on the hills overlooking the city
just thinking about time.
I'm thinking about my successes and failures over the
years
and even though I am not an aged woman
I am a young woman who has experienced many trials.
Some say the older you get, the more you learn from
life's disappointments.
I think it is important to know that is just what they are
– disappointments.
But how do we keep moving?
How do we keep going when hurdles are constantly
placed in our paths?
Education? Maybe.
Money? Can change things but it doesn't bring
happiness.
Spirituality? Only if you believe
and I wonder just how far my faith can go
Perhaps farther than the winds that blow
but at times, it has its highs and lows
its cold fronts and warm breezes
that puts my mind at ease.
Still, who is there for me?
When honesty and integrity are put on the line,
who will stand up?
No wonder at times I like solitude because there is
no reading in between the lines, mixed interpretations,
backbiting, and lies.

As I sit here and meditate and express these thoughts
I know that they will not come back to haunt me
because solitude has no feelings except peace
I love this time to just sit still and think.
Though solitude is my friend at times, I still get lonely
That's just one of life's disappointments.
But like the wind that blows,
we see how time goes
and with each problem, we can grow.
As I overlook the city at the small dotted people,
they have their own problems too.
We are all in this world together.
Even though we differ with circumstances
some great, others small, we are all in this together.
And in some place, somewhere out there, somebody is
sitting on the hills overlooking the city like me, feeling
the winds that pass us by...

The Little Things

We were sitting in the park
Near the lake
Feeding the birds
with bread before it got too late
The sun was setting
We were talking for hours
laughing, joking, nothing was sour
I never knew you were so honest and frank
I felt comfortable in your arms and there I sank
When we finished talking, you kissed me well
But it wasn't just a kiss, it had meaning and bliss
Only knowing each other a short time, I would
remember this
We discussed it all, with no shame or nothing
to cause the conscious to crawl
I would never look at you the same way again
At first, being a man who was just my friend
I never felt so vulnerable, but you assured me it was
okay
You held my hand gently, and caressed it with your
face
I wanted to hold on
so the night would never end
I wanted to start the day all over again
but I knew I couldn't, still I felt so free
just sitting in your arms
knowing you discovered me.

Knowing

There are so many things we want to say
But we don't
Sometimes pride holds us back
Or fear of what one may say back
Or just not wanting to feel soft in a world that's so cold.
Who wants to be vulnerable?
So, what's the use in pressing on?
If you want to go, then be gone

Knowing that's not what I want
But the previous hurt makes me front
Now that I look back
I really wanted you to know that
Maybe I just wasn't ready back then
Knowing.

Pigeon Poop

I tried to see, but I couldn't
Hair was sprawled over my face
I saw a fly land on my pudding.
Mama tugged and pulled. She said, "We have to clean
the kitchen."
A mosquito bit my neck, and I couldn't stop itching.
Mama combed, brushed, clipped, and tied.
I cried and cried, and wondered why as birds flew by
my nest.
Pain was beauty, and beauty was pain.
The stroke of luck came from the bird's dripping.
Pretty ole pretty is how Mama made me
She fixed my hair and set me free, but baby bird
pooped all over me.
"They call it luck," Mama said, but I didn't feel so lucky
when she had to start all over again.

Love's Mirage

My lover of my dreams
Come to me in ecstasy for my fantasy and life's dream.
To you, my lover, I know this is real. I'm emotional in
constant motion as I try to keep still, and wait for the
surprise.
I'm in love with your eyes. A pool of sea green blue. My
lover of my dreams, please come true.
Lightly as you touch me, I am still.
Patient you are and careful you are
as you tempt to love me, not fast,
the lover of my dreams, go slow to make it last.
To you, my lover, I surrender my soul, as you discover
new places within me I never thought I could go. As I
love you, uncontrollably losing my sane, and when it
ends, I'm thinking of how I can love you all over again.
To you, my love, I want you to awaken me from this
dream, and show me all of what your love can truly
bring.

Streams

Old letters tossed in boxed storage
adding to the photographs there
almost the last of the mementos
except for the memories inside my head
Some thoughts can be depressing
the happier ones fondly linger,
but not too long
it gets like a scratched song, and that can be a stinker!
Not really admiring gypsies
with them, no goals are born
but in my travels with life's streams
after trials, you move on.
With goals of finding new people,
new places, and walking new roads
all can be as smooth as streams if you let old things
stay old.
I've learned that streams always pass over
the rocky things underneath
allowing me to look beyond the surface
but keep moving ahead, while the past stays below my
feet.

Venus Stood Bright

We held on to each other
So close
We were afraid of letting go
Letting go meant goodbye
And new beginnings
Our relationship was ending
I loved you so much
I wanted to live inside you
That way, I would always be there to guide you
I cried my last tear
And you wiped my eyes
I saw Venus standing bright in the sky.
Goodbye.

(This poem is two poems put together to make one and can
also be read in reverse.)

You are My Poetry

The east coast has its change of seasons
from winter around to spring,
and we've had our ups and downs but survived
everything.
The sea has its waves, and you know just how to
soothe my tough, high energetic, and melancholy
moods.
The rainbow has many colors, fading in between
the clouds; it's the symbol of our future, and it always
makes me smile.
The air we feel is always there
everlasting and keeps us strong
Though we cannot see it like we can't see God
He helps us to carry on.
Diamonds and pearls are precious jewels
but they are hard to find
like the right man to be my husband
is as good as fine wine.
You have become my poetry, and all the lyrics I write.
You are my poetry, my eternal love for life.

Eclipse

Our love was like an eclipse
It came so fast it almost blinded me
From its shining sun to the dark pale moon,
I went from loving to despising you, and my heart
regretted wasting energy on you.
Our love was like an eclipse
I should have turned away when I heard the warning
but hoped things would change
Soon I saw the significance of the sun and moon as
they returned to their rightful place, and I wished our
paths had never crossed in the first place.

Maturity

If you pick a bud too early
You'll never see it bloom.
If I pick you right now, it would be too soon.
If you eat a tomato right before it's ripe,
the taste would be bittersweet like now
if you were in my life.

Since I'm a full-grown flower
I can't wait for other buds to mature.
Because I don't know when the time will come
for you to reach that core.
As for the tomatoes,
I always prefer mine to be sweet.
If I put my love on you now,
I would sweep you off your feet
Before you're ready.

Think About It

I'm the funk in your guitar
The beat of your drums
The notes on your keyboards
But still, you can't score
Cuz your pitch is off tune
And you're not cool
Like a rhyme in a poem
My lyrics are smooth
You can't handle my music of rhythm and blues.

I'm the sole on your shoes,
The clamp on your watch,
The twist in your locks, but you can't stop
For once and say
without her, there is no me.
Think about it!

If My Heart Had Wings

If my heart had wings
I'd love for it to fly
and sit and chill with you
and rest by your side.
It would learn your every emotion
and what you feel deep inside.
It would lie with you, and watch you
fall asleep, and dance all night long to
the rhythm of your heartbeat.

If my heart had wings, it would be free
from feeling pain.
It would fly away
from the emotions working up in your soul
so it wouldn't be to blame
but it would understand those who never felt
understood, and give them affection like no human
could.
But one day, the heart would fall in love and join the
human body again
because it would have learned to love
from the outside and in.

Regrets

I used to have this deep silence
that rested inside of me
a part of calmness I felt
not only when I'd sleep
It rested like a snowflake
in the center of my heart
and nothing seemed to bother
or tear the peace apart
until I started considering advice
from worldly friends
not trusting my own intuition or God
who was my true friend
Like a loud noise something erupted from within
confusion brought on by sorrow and my happiness
came to an end
then when it was over
I wanted back that restful state,
But it will take some time, I know,
I just hope it's not too late.

Bloom of Youth

Your young heart cannot be trusting
in your moments of feelings for me.
For you are like a splendor of grass
young, energetic, but naïve.
In your mind, you dream of me
with every fantasy you want fulfilled.
My tears are saved in a bottle for you.
I wish I could grant your will.
But why should I stay caught up in your infatuating
wants?
And torture my seasoned heart
to go backward instead of forward
I beg of you little bud
to let yourself grow
and not hurry in your developments
like other flowers, you'll grow.

Reunited

That old familiar scent
When your lips touched mine
and your arms held me like forever.
I remember when I never thought this moment would
come again
A distant past refurbished like an antique chair with
minor repairs made here and there.
This is a new chapter to start together again
with a few leftover pieces from our history to make it
all authentic again.

Good Enough

Critical people are never satisfied
Neither are the analytical trusting
Some people are always stuck in the past and can never
draw a straight line
And not even I can make the critical ones happy
nor the analytical ones believe
I can only be me
even if my ALL
isn't good enough
for them.

Learning to Love Again

Loving you
is a reality to someday let you go
I am guarded and distant
but I told you so.
You can bid on a horse
but it may not run fast
So perhaps it's a trust thing
I wonder if this will last
I'm honest
with you
with me
and with love
but not complete,
it just takes too long
for my heart to heal
after it's been beat.
This pace is moderate
steady
and not too fast
so I can use good judgment
this time around
and not love too fast.
Let your love be a raging bull
knocking down the door to my heart
when you chose me
you chose a challenge
so finish what you start.

My Life

She was the Eighth Wonder of the World
seeded by an Opal, birthed by the Garnet
a precious baby girl.

Coming last to the Ruby in June
a Luna of aqua metamorphosis
dancing a melodic tune.

A dimpled femme fatale
blossoming into a butterfly
A cosmic of the 70s
bell bottoms and SuperFly.

Bye-bye, boogie baby
It's on to the crazy 80s
of Jupiter and space beats
moonwalking, pop-locking
jellybean shoes on her feet.

She got five-cent pop rock candy
candy rings and orange Push-Ups
Runs back home from her father's store
to play freeze tag and Double Dutch.

E.T. phoning home
graced the cover of her lunchbox
Braided cornrows with colorful beads
she bopped her head to the boombox.

Come on Vogue, strike a pose
She was a 90s teen
with blue jeans and party shirts
a House Music scene.

Falling for a heart of the same month,
first time in love
stringing a guitar of purple ribbon
bonded like a hand in a glove.

Caps and gowns in blue
Class of '92
She completed the big E.
And went off to another chapter in life
at Smith University.

Time moving fast and spinning forward
The Spirit drawing her near
through times ancient book of prophecy,
a pool to get baptized in.

Without looking back,
she made the sacrifice
surrendering to her Heavenly Father
and the Day Star
with hopes of a better tomorrow, and everlasting life,
she would hold close to her heart.

A Mother's Love

Doctors said it was all normal
but certainly it wasn't to you
They weren't there when you had to give him air as he
started to turn blue.
So forgive me for being the way I am
a very protective mom who wants no harm
that's just the way that I am.
I prayed to God for a baby
and I am still thankful for what He gave me
I love my son so much that at times my worries drive
me crazy.
There's nothing like having a sick child
My heart would bleed tears from a broken valve.
Today I thank Jehovah and Jesus that he's all better
now!

The Colors of My Mind

I'm just a middle-aged woman
but some days I feel 100 years old
It's all apart of what I'm going through
with the butterfly being gone.

Some say I'm just lazy
but there are things they just can't see
like when I'm smiling on the outside
there are tears inside of me.

In the mornings when I look in the mirror,
I remember what used to be
I once had all of my eyebrows, hair, and lashes
but this condition took control over me.

I used to cry almost every night and beg God to take
this away
I used to feel so angry at the world because this is never
going away.

I read a quote one day that said, *What you can't
change, you must accept.*
That was the day I stood in the path of courage and
refused to see my death.
I may be changing on the outside, but I'm still the same
within.
I've never been one to quit on anything, and I'd much
rather win.

I'm still a loving and compassionate person, and I love
to have a ball, but sometimes my condition limits me,
but I refuse to fall.

I wrote this book of poems, not to reflect on what used
to be
But for you to understand the colors of my mind are
the colors that still make me, ME.